Presented

To Danielle White

Date 12/06/2005

Trust in the Lord ~ John 14:1

sov AS09

Presented to

_____

by

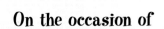

_____

On the occasion of

_____

Jesus and Me

Text by **Nina Smit**

Illustrations by **Rassie Erasmus**

CANDLE
BOOKS

Contents

Old Testament

New Testament

To help you get started

This book has been written to help you make your quiet time with God very special. Each daily reading has five parts:

❑ A thought to ponder or a question for you to answer to make your Bible story for the day easier to understand;

❑ A Bible story you can read for yourself;

❑ Something God wants you to know;

❑ A short prayer so that you can talk to God, and

❑ A short Bible verse that you can learn by heart.

Old Testament

The story of creation

Think carefully: *Have you ever made something of which you were very proud? What do you need when you want to make something out of plasticine or build a Lego aeroplane?*

Read: Many, many years ago, there was no sky and no earth. Can you imagine that? But God has always been there. One day, God decided to make a heaven and an earth.

What God wants me to know: *God is the Creator of all things.*

On the first day He made light, on the second day the white clouds and the blue sea. On the third day God made green trees and plants; on the fourth day the yellow sun, the moon, and the bright stars; on the fifth day the fishes and the birds; and on the sixth day He made all the animals.

When God saw all the things He had made, He was happy, because everything was beautiful and good.

When you want to make a little plasticine animal or a Lego model, you need plasticine or Lego. But God made all the wonderful things on earth out of nothing. He is the Creator of all things.

What I can say to God: *Lord, thank You for making the world so beautiful. Thank You for light and clouds, for the sun and moon and stars, for trees and flowers, fishes and birds, and for the many kinds of animals. Amen.*

Find the story in Genesis Chapter 1

Learn by heart: "*God looked at everything he had made, and he was very pleased.*" (Genesis 1:31)

11

God made you

Think carefully: *Do you remember the things God made on the first six days? (Go back to yesterday's reading if you have forgotten.) Now there was a sun, a moon, stars, plants, and animals on earth. What was still missing?*

Read: After God had made the sun and moon and stars, trees and plants, fishes and birds and animals, one thing was still missing, so God took some dust from the ground and made the first man. This person was the most wonderful of all the things He had made, because God made man in His image. He had a heart and a soul and a mind, just like God Himself. Unlike the animals, the man could talk to God and love God.

    Even today, you are just like the first person God made. God also gave you a mind and a soul so that you can talk to Him and love Him. Because God made you, He loves you very much and dearly wants you to be His child.

What God wants me to know:
You are the most wonderful thing that God has made.

What I can say to God: *Thank You for making me so special. Thank You that I can see and hear and play. Thank You that I may love You because You are great and good. Amen.*

Find the story in Genesis Chapter 1 verses 26–31

Learn by heart: *"He made us, and we belong to him."*
(Psalm 100:3)

Adam and Eve

Think carefully: *Do you always do everything your mother and father ask you to do? What do your parents do when you are disobedient?*

Read: Adam and Eve were very happy living in the garden of Eden. They were allowed to eat fruit from all the trees, except the fruit from the tree growing in the middle of the garden. One day the devil told Eve they would not die if they ate fruit from that tree. He said the fruit would make them just as clever as God.

Eve was disobedient. She picked the fruit and ate it, and she gave Adam some too. That was very wrong. God had to punish them because they were disobedient. They had to leave the garden of Eden. But God promised them that one day He would send Someone who would be stronger than the devil. Do you know who that was?

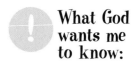

What God wants me to know: *All people are sinners, but Jesus paid the price for our sin on the cross.*

What I can say to God: *Thank You, God, for sending Jesus to take the punishment for my sins. Please forgive me when I am disobedient. Amen.*

Find the story in Genesis Chapters 2 – 3

Learn by heart: *"Everyone has sinned and is far away from God's saving presence."* (Romans 3:23)

Noah builds an ark

 Think carefully: *Have you ever seen a rainbow when the rain stops? Read in Genesis 9:11-16 what God promised Noah.*

Read: God was sad because the people sinned so much. He had to punish them. But there was one man whom God loved. His name was Noah. God told Noah to build a big ark. It had to be big enough for Noah and his whole family to live in, as well as a male and female of each kind of animal in the world.

"I am going to bring a flood and everybody will drown," God told Noah. "But you and your family will be safe inside the ark."

 When Noah had finished building the ark, it began to rain. It rained for forty days and nights—everything was flooded. Only Noah's ark floated on top of the water.

When the water dried up, Noah and his family and the animals came out of the ark. They were very grateful to God for saving them from the flood.

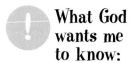 **What God wants me to know:** *God punishes sin, but He always protects His children.*

 What I can say to God: *Heavenly Father, thank You for the beautiful rainbow after the rain. Thank You for watching over me and for protecting me. Amen.*

Find the story in Genesis Chapters 6 – 9

Learn by heart: *"It was faith that made Noah hear God's warnings."*
(Hebrews 11:7)

The tower of Babel

Think carefully: *In the United Kingdom we hear many languages: English, German, French and many others. Can you understand more than one language?*

Read: In the beginning, all the people on earth spoke the same language. Then they got together and said: "Let's build a city with a high tower that reaches all the way to heaven. Then we will be very important, and we can always live together."

The Lord listened to them boasting among themselves. He saw that they no longer loved Him. He decided to stop them.

Suddenly, all the people started speaking in different languages. They could not understand one another at all, so they had to stop building the high tower and the big city.

After that, they went to live in different places. The people were spread out over the whole world.

What God wants me to know: *It is wrong when people think they are just as important as God.*

What I can say to God: *Lord, thank You that I may love You. Thank You that I may talk to You in my own language. Amen.*

Find the story in Genesis Chapter 11

Learn by heart: *"Never forget that the Lord is God. He made us, and we belong to him"* (Psalm 100:3)

Abram and Lot

Think carefully: *What do you do when your friends come to play and your mother gives you cake? Do you take the biggest piece, or do you let them choose first?*

Read: Abram and his nephew Lot lived in the same place. But it was not big enough for both of them. Their herdsmen were forever arguing with one another, so Abram said to Lot: "Let's not have any more arguing, for we are relatives. If you go to the left, I'll go to the right; if you go to the right, I'll go to the left."

Actually, Abram should have chosen first, because he was the oldest. But Abram was God's child. He always gave the best to other people.

Lot chose the best part of the land for himself. He went to live in the valley of Jordan, while Abram remained in the land of Canaan.

The Lord was pleased with Abram. "All the land that you see I will give to you and your offspring," He said to Abram.

What God wants me to know: *God's children always give the best to others.*

What I can say to God: *Heavenly Father, I'm sorry if I'm selfish sometimes and don't share my toys and sweets with my friends. Please make me as unselfish as Abram. Amen.*

Find the story in Genesis Chapter 13

Learn by heart: *"Do for others what you want them to do for you."*
(Matthew 7:12)

Abraham and Sarah

Think carefully: *Do you like waiting and waiting for something? Or do you become impatient, especially when it takes a long time before God answers your prayers?*

Read: God promised Abraham and his wife Sarah a baby son. He said that they would have as many children as the stars in the heavens and the grains of sand along the seashore.

But the years passed and they did not have a child. By this time Abraham and his wife were very old. Perhaps they thought God had forgotten about His promise.

Although they had to wait such a long time, God kept His word. He always does what He promises. Abraham and Sarah did have a baby—they were very happy and called the baby Isaac.

Sometimes God makes you wait a long time before He answers your prayers. He wants to see if you really believe in His promises.

What God wants me to know: *Sometimes you will wait a long time before your prayers are answered. But God always keeps His promises.*

What I can say to God: *Thank You, God, that You always do what You have promised. Thank You for listening when I pray. Help me to wait patiently for Your answer. Amen.*

Find the story in Genesis Chapters 17 – 18, 21

Learn by heart: *"Trust in the Lord now and forever!"*
(Psalm 131:3)

Abraham and Isaac

Think carefully: *Have you taken tests at your school yet? Tests are not always pleasant, but they help your teacher to find out how much you have learned during the year.*

Read: Abraham loved his son Isaac very much because he had to wait such a long time to have him. But Abraham loved God even more than his son. One day God asked Abraham to do a terrible thing. "Abraham," He said, "I want you to sacrifice your son to Me." Abraham was very sad, but immediately made preparations. Early the next morning he and Isaac went to the mountain where he was to sacrifice his son.

God saw that Abraham was obedient to Him. He had passed his test! As Abraham was about to sacrifice Isaac, God said: "Leave your son! Now I know that you want to serve Me."

Abraham looked up and saw a ram caught by its horns in a bush. He sacrificed the ram to God instead of his son.

What God wants me to know:

Sometimes you may have a hard time. That is the time God is testing your love for Him.

What I can say to God: *Lord, thank You that You are always with me and that You help me when I am in trouble. Help me always to love You more than anyone else. Amen.*

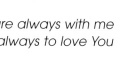

Find the story in Genesis Chapter 22

Learn by heart: *"For you know that when your faith succeeds in facing such trials, the result is the ability to endure."* (James 1:3)

Jacob and Esau

Think carefully: *Have you ever lied to anyone? We all tell fibs at one time or another—but God thinks this is very, very wrong.*

Read: Abraham's son Isaac had twin sons. Their names were Jacob and Esau. Esau liked hunting, but Jacob preferred staying at home. He was his mother's favourite. Isaac had become old, blind, and sickly. He asked Esau, his older son, to shoot a deer for him and to prepare the meat so that he could bless him before he died.

Rebekah, Isaac's wife, wanted Jacob to receive the blessing, so she quickly cooked two goats and covered Jacob's neck and hands with the goat skins so that Isaac would mistake him for Esau. When Isaac felt the hairy hands, he gave Jacob the blessing that should have been Esau's.

When Esau returned with a deer for his father and found out what had happened, he was so angry that he wanted to kill Jacob. Jacob had to run for his life.

What God wants me to know: *You can hide things from people, but God knows everything about you.*

What I can say to God: *Lord, please help me always to be honest. Thank You for knowing me so well and for still loving me. Amen.*

Find the story in Genesis Chapters 25, 27

Learn by heart: *"Speak the truth to one another."*
(Zechariah 8:16)

Joseph and his brothers

Think carefully: *Do you sometimes feel that your mother and father love your brother or sister more than they love you? How do you feel about that?*

What God wants me to know: *God loves all His children equally. He never loves one person more than another.*

Read: Jacob had twelve sons. He loved Joseph most and had a beautiful robe made for him. Joseph's brothers were very angry about this. They were jealous because their father favoured Joseph, so they made sly plans to teach Joseph a lesson.

At first they wanted to kill him, but Reuben, the oldest brother, wanted to save Joseph and stopped them. "Let's not kill him. Throw him in that well instead," said Reuben. His brothers listened to him and threw Joseph into the well. When Reuben left, they took him out of the well and sold him to some travellers. Eventually Joseph was sold as a slave in Egypt. His brothers told their father that a wild animal had killed Joseph. Jacob was very sad.

What I can say to God: *Heavenly Father, thank You for loving me just as much as You love everyone else. Please help me to be patient with my brothers and sisters. Amen.*

Find the story in Genesis Chapter 37

Learn by heart: *"God judges everyone by the same standard."*
(Colossians 3:25)

Moses in the reed basket

Think carefully: *Are you sometimes asked to look after your baby sister or brother? Do you enjoy doing that?*

Read: The king of Egypt treated the Israelites very badly. He made them work hard all day, and he gave an order to have all baby boys put to death. One day, one of the women thought of a clever plan to save her baby son's life. She wove a basket from reeds, put the baby inside, and hid the basket and the baby in the reeds by the river. Miriam, the baby's sister, had to look after him.

What God wants me to know: *God protects all His children, and He has a special plan for each one of us.*

When the king's daughter came to swim in the river, she found the baby hidden in the reeds. Miriam offered to bring her mother to nurse that baby until he was big enough. The princess loved the baby Moses very much, and he grew up in the palace. God had a plan for this baby. One day, he would lead His people out of Egypt.

What I can say to God: *Heavenly Father, thank You for protecting me and keeping me safe from harm. Thank You that You have a plan for my life. Amen.*

Find the story in Exodus Chapters 1 - 2

Learn by heart: *"God says, 'I will save those who love me.'"*
(Psalm 91:14)

God saves His people

Think carefully: *God is with His children every day. He helps them and rescues them. Are you sure that God is always with you?*

Read: When Moses had grown up, God asked him to lead His people out of Egypt to the land He had prepared for them. At first, the king wouldn't allow them to leave, but after God had sent ten plagues, they were allowed to go.

They had hardly left when the king regretted having let them go. He sent soldiers after them to bring them back. The Israelites were very scared. Behind them were the Egyptians and in front of them lay the Red Sea. But God parted the sea so that they could pass through without even getting their feet wet!

When the Egyptians tried to follow them, the wall of water rushed over them and they all drowned. God always helps His children and saves them.

What God wants me to know: *God is almighty. He can do anything. He will always help you and save you.*

What I can say to God: *Heavenly Father, thank You that You can do anything. Thank You that I don't have to be afraid because You will always help me and save me. Amen.*

Find the story in Exodus Chapters 5 - 14

Learn by heart: "*The Lord is my strong defender; he is the one who has saved me.*" (Exodus 15:2)

God takes care of His people

Think carefully: *Do you sometimes get angry when you can't have everything you want? Do you believe that God will give you everything you need?*

Read: Once the Israelites felt safe in the desert, they quickly forgot how good God had been to them. In the desert, the food wasn't as good as it had been in Egypt. The Israelites went to Moses and complained: "Why did you make us leave Egypt? In this desert we are going to die of hunger and thirst."

Moses prayed to God, and God sent the people food from heaven. Hundreds of birds called quails covered the earth for the Israelites to kill and eat. Every morning they picked up flakes of manna from the ground. It looked like snow and tasted like honey. Now they had more than enough food. Yet they were still not satisfied.

What God wants me to know: *You should be grateful for everything God gives you.*

What I can say to God: *Lord, thank You for all the things You give me. Thank You that I have enough food and clothes. Help me not to complain about things. Amen.*

34

Find the story in Exodus Chapter 16

Learn by heart: *"My God will supply all your needs."*
(Philippians 4:19)

Moses becomes very angry

Think carefully: *Have you been very angry with your brother or sister? How do you feel when someone is angry with you?*

Read: Moses tried hard not to become too angry with the Israelites, but they were still complaining. "Give us water to drink, we are very thirsty," they complained. "Why did you make us leave Egypt to die of thirst here in the desert?"

When Moses heard this, he became very angry. "What must I do with these people?" he asked God.

"Take your brother Aaron's staff and speak to that rock and water will pour out of it," God told Moses.

Moses was so angry that he struck the rock very hard with the staff. Water gushed out of the rock. But God wasn't pleased with Moses. Because he had lost his temper, he would not be allowed to enter the promised land when the time came.

What God wants me to know: *God does not want His children to lose their temper.*

What I can say to God: *Lord, I'm sorry that I sometimes lose my temper when I get angry. Please give me peace in my heart. Amen.*

Find the story in Numbers Chapter 20

Learn by heart: *"Do not let your anger lead you into sin."* (Ephesians 4:26)

The talking donkey

Think carefully: *Do you want lots of money? Would you do something you know is wrong if someone gave you money to do it?*

What God wants me to know: *You must not love money more than you love God.*

Read: When Balak, king of Moab, saw that God had helped the Israelites in the war, he was very scared, so he asked the prophet Balaam to come and curse the Israelites. At first, Balaam did not want to do this. But when King Balak offered him lots of money, he decided to go with the messengers.

Balaam rode on his donkey, and God wanted to stop him. He sent an angel to stand in the road before Balaam. When the donkey saw the angel, he refused to walk any further. Balaam became so angry that he beat the donkey with a stick. He only saw the angel when the donkey began to speak to him. So Balaam blessed the Israelites as God had ordered him to do. King Balak was very angry about this.

What I can say to God: *Lord, please help me never to love money more than I love You. I will always listen to what You tell me. Amen.*

Find the story in Numbers Chapters 22 – 24

Learn by heart: *"For the love of money is a source of all kinds of evil."*
(1 Timothy 6:10)

The law of God: The ten commandments

? **Think carefully:** *Can you recite the ten commandments? If you can't, write them down neatly.*

Read: God loved Moses very much. He asked him to climb a high mountain because He wanted to speak to him there. Moses climbed higher and higher, until the Israelites could no longer see him. There was smoke and lightning over the mountain. The Israelites trembled with fear. God spoke to Moses.

! **What God wants me to know:** *God also wants you to obey each one of the ten commandments.*

Moses remained on the mountain with God for a long time. God gave Moses His law, the ten commandments. God wrote with His finger on two flat stone tablets. Moses had to explain the commandments to the people. They were to obey each of the commandments. If they obeyed, God would bless them and their children.

66 **What I can say to God:** *Lord, thank You for Your commandments. Thank You that they teach me how to live if I want to be happy. Help me to obey Your law. Amen.*

Find the story in Exodus Chapter 20

Learn by heart: *"Love the Lord your God and always obey all his laws."*
(Deuteronomy 11:1)

Love the Lord your God

Think carefully: *Which of the ten commandments do you think is the most important?*

What God wants me to know: *You must love God more than anybody else.*

Read: On the first stone tablet that God gave to Moses, He wrote the four commandments that tell us to love God more than anyone else. Listen to them carefully:

You may not have other gods.
You may not make idols and worship them.
You may not misuse the name of God.
You must put aside a special day for God.

The two most important things God wants to teach you in His law are that you must love God very much, and that you must love other people. Because you are sinful, you can't do that by yourself. But you can ask God to help you. Will you try?

What I can say to God: *Heavenly Father, thank You that I may love You. Will You please help me to obey Your law? Amen.*

Find the story in Exodus 20 verses 1-8

Learn by heart: *"Love the Lord your God with all your heart."*
(Luke 10:27)

You must love others

Think carefully: *Can you still remember the two most important things the law of God teaches us?*

Read: On the second stone tablet God gave to Moses, He wrote the commandments that teach us to love others as much as we love ourselves. Listen to them carefully:

> You must listen to your parents.
> You may not kill other people.
> Husbands and wives must keep their marriage promise.
> You may not take something that belongs to someone else.
> You may not tell lies.
> You may not be jealous of other people.

What God wants me to know: *God wants you to love other people as much as you love yourself.*

If you can manage to love all other people as much as you love yourself, it will be easy for you to obey these last six commandments. When you love other people, you won't lie to them, take their things or be jealous of them. Ask God to help you to love other people as much as you love yourself.

What I can say to God: *Heavenly Father, I will really try my best to love other people. Thank You for loving me. Amen.*

Find the story in Exodus Chapter 20 verses 12–17

Learn by heart: *"Love your neighbour as you love yourself."*
(Matthew 22:39)

Achan is dishonest

Think carefully: *What do you do when you find something that doesn't belong to you? Have you ever copied from a friend's homework?*

Read: God helped His people to win many wars. The people of Jericho, one of the cities against which the Israelites fought, worshipped idols. God ordered Joshua to burn everything that remained of the city. But Achan, one of the soldiers, was dishonest. He took some of the city people's clothes, as well as silver and gold, and buried them in his tent.

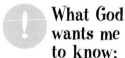

What God wants me to know:

You must listen to God, and you may not take things that don't belong to you.

This made God very angry, and the Israelites lost the war against the city of Ai. When Joshua asked God why they had lost, He told Joshua that some of the forbidden things had been stolen. Achan admitted that he had taken these things. Joshua sent for the stolen goods and Achan and his family were put to death.

What I can say to God: *Lord, I am sorry that I am sometimes disobedient and do the wrong thing. Will You please forgive me? Amen.*

Find the story in Joshua Chapter 7

Learn by heart: *"Do not steal."* (Exodus 20:15)

Gideon, the brave hero

Think carefully: *Have you ever managed to do something that was very difficult because God helped you? Tell one of your friends about it today.*

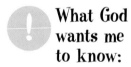

Read: Because the Israelites refused to listen to God, He allowed the Midianites to win the war against them. The Israelites suffered greatly after that. Then they remembered God again and asked Him to help them.

God sent His angel to Gideon. "You must rescue the people from the might of the Midianites," the angel told Gideon. "God will be with you."

Gideon wanted to take many soldiers, but God allowed him to choose only 300. Because God was with them, Gideon and his 300 men defeated the Midianites' big army. With God on your side, you can do anything.

What God wants me to know:

You can do anything if God gives you the strength to do it.

What I can say to God: *Lord, thank You for being with me every day. Thank You that I know I can overcome any problems with Your help. Amen.*

Find the story in Judges Chapters 6 – 7

Learn by heart: *"I have the strength to face all conditions by the power that Christ gives me."* (Philippians 4:13)

Samson, the strong man

Think carefully: *Have you ever promised somebody something and not kept your promise? Do you think it is right to break a promise?*

Read: Samson was devoted to God from the moment he was born. God loved him very much. He blessed Samson and made him very strong, so that he could deliver God's people from the might of the Philistines. Samson's secret was that he should never cut off his hair.

Unfortunately, Samson fell in love with a woman who was a heathen. Her name was Delilah. The Philistines bribed her to find out Samson's secret. She nagged him until he gave in and broke his promise to God. He told her that his strength lay in his hair. Delilah cut off Samson's hair while he slept. This made it possible for the Philistines to capture him. But Samson's hair grew again. With God's help he would still kill many Philistines.

What God wants me to know: *God expects you to keep your promises, just as He keeps every one of His promises.*

What I can say to God: *Lord, thank You for always doing what You have promised. I am sorry that I have not always kept my promises to my friends. Help me always to keep my promises. Amen.*

Find the story in Judges Chapters 13 – 16

Learn by heart: *"I have hidden Your word in my heart."*
(Psalm 119:11 NIV)

The Lord talks to Samuel

 Think carefully: *Has God ever talked to you? How does God talk to His children today?*

Read: Samuel was still very young. He helped Eli the priest in the temple. Samuel loved God very much. One night Samuel woke up and heard someone calling him. He got up immediately and ran to Eli's room. "Here I am; you called me," he said to Eli. "I didn't call you, go back to sleep," Eli said. Twice more Samuel heard someone calling him.

The third time he went to Eli's room, Eli realised that it was God who wanted to talk to Samuel.

When Samuel heard the voice again, he said: "Speak, Lord, Your servant is listening!" Samuel listened to God and did what God asked him to do. Even today, God is talking to you when you read the Bible and when you go to church.

What God wants me to know: *God still talks to His children today when they read the Bible and go to church.*

 What I can say to God: *Thank You for talking to me when I read my Bible. Help me to be like Samuel and always obey You. Amen.*

Find the story in 1 Samuel Chapter 3

Learn by heart: *"Speak, Lord, Your servant is listening."*
(1 Samuel 3:9)

David and Jonathan

Think carefully: *Who is your very best friend? Have you ever done anything to help that friend?*

What God wants me to know:
It is good to have friends—friends should always help each other.

Read: David and king Saul's son Jonathan were best friends. King Saul did not like this at all. He was very jealous of David because he was so brave and because everybody liked him. He was afraid that one day David would take his place as king. Quietly, he decided to have David killed. But Jonathan heard of his father's plans and warned David.

Because Jonathan and David loved each other, Jonathan wanted to protect David from his father's evil plan. David was able to escape and Saul could not find him.

Saul was very angry, but David never forgot that Jonathan had saved his life.

What I can say to God: *Heavenly Father, thank You for all my friends. Please show me how I can help them. Amen.*

Find the story in 1 Samuel Chapters 19 – 20

Learn by heart: *"A friend loves at all times."* (Proverbs 17:17 NIV)

Solomon, the wisest king

 Think carefully: *If you could choose to be anything you liked, what would you choose? Would you like to be very wise?*

Read: David's son Solomon became king of Israel. God loved Solomon very much. One day He asked Solomon: "What would you like Me to give you?" "I am still young, and have to rule my people," Solomon answered. "Help me always to know what is right and what is wrong."

 Solomon wanted wisdom so that he could be a good king to his people. God was pleased with this answer. He made Solomon the wisest king ever. He also gave him wealth, fame, and a long life. Solomon ruled over Israel for forty years. He was very rich and famous. People came from all over the world to listen to his wisdom.

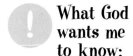 **What God wants me to know:** *You can also ask God to show you what is right and what is wrong.*

 What I can say to God: *Lord, thank You for giving me a mind. Please help me to know what is wrong and what is right. Amen.*

Find the story in 1 Kings Chapter 3

Learn by heart: *"But if any of you lacks wisdom, he should pray to God, who will give it to him."* (James 1:5)

57

Elijah and the ravens

? **Think carefully:** *Do you believe that God can perform miracles? Have you ever heard of a miracle that happened?*

Read: The prophet Elijah told king Ahab that God would bring a drought over the land because the people would not listen to Him. God ordered Elijah to go to the brook of Cherith. God said: "You may drink water from the stream, and I will send ravens to bring you food."

Elijah did this. Every morning and every evening the ravens brought him bread and meat. Don't you think that is wonderful? Elijah drank water from the stream until the stream dried up.

Later, God sent Elijah to Zarephath. He went to live with a widow there, and God provided for them until the drought had passed.

! **What God wants me to know:**

God never leaves His children in the lurch. He still performs miracles as He did in the time of Elijah.

" **What I can say to God:** *Heavenly Father, thank You for taking care of my needs every day. Please be with all the people who have no food to eat today. Amen.*

Find the story in 1 Kings Chapter 17

Learn by heart: *I will honour you and praise your name. You have done amazing things.*" (Isaiah 25:1)

Naaman is healed

Think carefully: *Do you find it difficult to talk to your friends about God? He wants His children to talk about Him.*

Read: Naaman was the commander of the army of the king of Aram. He was a brave, important man. Then he contracted leprosy. A young girl, who had been taken captive from Israel, worked for Naaman's wife. She said to him: "Our God can do everything. If you could find our prophet Elisha, he would heal you."

Naaman immediately tried to find Elisha. When he found him, Elisha sent him a message: "Go and wash yourself seven times in the river Jordan, and you will be healed."

After doing that, Naaman was completely healed. He was very happy and offered Elisha a generous gift, but Elisha refused it. From that day on, Naaman worshipped God.

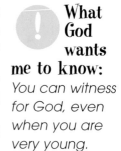

What God wants me to know: *You can witness for God, even when you are very young.*

What I can say to God: *Heavenly Father, thank You for letting me be Your child. Please help me to tell all my friends how much I love You. Amen.*

Find the story in 2 Kings Chapter 5

Learn by heart: *"Go, then, to all peoples everywhere and make them My disciples."* (Matthew 28:19)

King Josiah

? **Think carefully:** *How old are you? Do you think a person can be a king if he is only eight years old?*

Read: King Josiah was only eight years old when he became king. Although he was so young, he was a good king. His mother was a good woman and she taught him well right from the beginning. Josiah did the same things as the great king David had done. God was very pleased with him.

One of the good things Josiah did, was to rebuild the house of God. He also found the Book of the Law in the temple. When he read this Book of the Law, Josiah realised how much his people had sinned. It made him so sad that he tore his clothing. God listened to him and promised not to punish the people while he was their king.

! **What God wants me to know:** *You can do important things for God, even though you are very young.*

" **What I can say to God:** *Lord, I really want to work for You, even though I am still young. Will You please show me what I can do for You? Amen.*

Find the story in 2 Kings Chapter 22

Learn by heart: *"Remember your Creator while you are still young."*
(Ecclesiastes 12:1)

The Lord is your shepherd

Think carefully: *Are you satisfied with what you have, or are there still many things you would like to have?*

Read: David wrote many psalms in which he tells us how good God is to His children. Psalm 23 tells us that God looks after us like a shepherd cares for his flocks.

David used to look after his father's sheep. He knew that a shepherd loves his sheep, gives them food, protects them from harm, and that the sheep follow the shepherd because they know his voice.

If the Lord is your shepherd, you will never want for anything. Even today, He still looks after every one of His children. And because He looks after you, you don't have to be afraid of anything. He protects you and promises that one day you will be in heaven with Him.

Have you made God your shepherd? Do you listen to His voice? Are you prepared to do what He asks you to do?

What God wants me to know: *God wants to be your shepherd and take care of you for the rest of your life.*

What I can say to God: *Heavenly Father, thank You for being my shepherd, and for taking such good care of me. Thank You that I have everything I need. I want to listen to You and follow You. Amen.*

Find the story in Psalm 23

Learn by heart: *"The Lord is my shepherd; I have everything I need."*
(Psalm 23:1)

Get to know your Bible

Think carefully: *Have you read your Bible from beginning to end and underlined all the verses you like? Wouldn't you like to do that?*

Read: Psalm 119 tells us how wonderful God's Word is. The Bible is God's Word; it is His letter to His children. When we read the Bible, we hear God's voice. God still talks to us through His Word, even though we cannot hear His voice with our ears. When we read the Bible, we hear what God wants to say to us.

Your Bible is a precious book. Read from it every day — in the morning before you get up and at night before you go to sleep. The Bible is like a lamp that shows you how God wants you to live. In His Bible, God teaches you what you should do, and warns you about things you should not do. Are you prepared to listen to what God is saying to you in His Word?

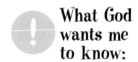

What God wants me to know: *God talks to His children when they read their Bible.*

What I can say to God: *Heavenly Father, thank You that I have my own Bible. Thank You for talking to me through Your Word. Help me to listen to Your voice and to love Your Word. Amen.*

Find the story in Psalm 119

Learn by heart: *"Your word is a lamp to guide me and a light for my path."* (Psalm 119:105)

God never sleeps

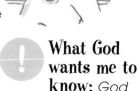

Think carefully: *Have you ever tried to stay awake all night? Do you think that it would be easy?*

Read: Psalm 121 is a song people sang on their way to God's temple in Jerusalem. To get there, they had to travel through a dangerous mountain pass. There were robbers on the road who attacked them. It was also very hot during the day. These travellers asked God to protect them on the road.

God still protects each of His children when they are in danger. We can talk to Him at any time of the day or night and ask Him to help us.

Psalm 121:4 tells us that God never sleeps. If you are scared at night when your parents are asleep, you can talk to God — He is always there to listen to you.

What God wants me to know: *God never sleeps—you can talk to Him any time of the day or night. He will always protect you.*

What I can say to God: *Lord, thank You for always being there when I need You. Thank You for never sleeping and for protecting me every day and night. Amen.*

Find the story in Psalm 121

Learn by heart: *"The Lord is by your side to protect you."*
(Psalm 121:5)

You are safe with the Lord

Think carefully: *Do you have a baby sister or brother? Have you watched the baby falling asleep in your mother's arms?*

Read: If there is a baby in your home, you must often have watched him or her falling asleep in your mother's arms. Babies usually stop crying when their mothers cradle them in their arms. They know that they are completely safe with their mothers, because a mother will always look after and protect her baby. Psalm 131 says that God's children can feel just as safe with God as a baby does with his or her mother.

Sometimes things happen to you that you don't understand. Perhaps someone in your home is very sick, or your grandma or grandad has died, or your dad has lost his job. Such things would make you feel unhappy and scared. But you don't have to worry, because whatever happens, you can tell God all about your problems. He will hold you in His arms and help you. He will always bring peace and calm to His children!

What God wants me to know: *With God you are always safe. He looks after you just as a mother looks after her baby.*

What I can say to God: *Lord, thank You for making me feel safe with You. Thank You that I have nothing to fear, because You hold me in Your arms. Amen.*

Find the story in Psalm 131

Learn by heart: *"My heart is quiet within me."* (Psalm 131:2)

Praise the Lord!

Think carefully: *Can you play a musical instrument? If you have one, you can praise the Lord with your music. If not, you can sing a song for the Lord because He makes you so happy.*

Read: In Psalm 150 the psalmist says all God's children must praise and worship Him. We can do this in different ways. We can play music for Him; we can sing to Him; or we can tell other people how good and wonderful He is.

Everything that breathes should praise the Lord. We must praise Him for all the wonderful things He does. We must praise Him because He loves us and cares for us. We must praise Him because He is great and good. All the praise and worship in our hearts is for Him, because there is no other God as wonderful as He is. How are you going to praise the Lord?

What God wants me to know: *God is pleased when His children worship and praise Him.*

What I can say to God: *Lord, there are so many things for which I can praise and worship You. I worship You because You made the world so beautiful. I worship You because You love me and care for me, and because You are great and mighty. Amen.*

72

Find the story in Psalm 150

Learn by heart: *"Praise the Lord, all living creatures!"* (Psalm 150:6)

Daniel in the den of lions

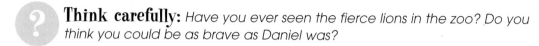

Think carefully: *Have you ever seen the fierce lions in the zoo? Do you think you could be as brave as Daniel was?*

Read: Daniel loved God. He prayed to God three times a day. The king of the heathen country liked Daniel very much. But there were bad people who were jealous of Daniel, so they urged the king to make a law saying that everybody had to worship the king and no other god. People who broke this law would be thrown in the lions' den.

Daniel took no notice of this law. He still prayed to God three times a day as usual, so the king had to have him thrown in the lions' den. But God sent an angel to protect Daniel. The next morning the king sent some of his men to take Daniel out of the den. From that day the heathen king began to worship Daniel's God.

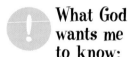

What God wants me to know: *If you are faithful to God, He will protect you from danger.*

What I can say to God: *Dear heavenly Father, thank You that I may talk to You each day just like Daniel. Thank You that I have nothing to fear because You will keep me from harm. Amen.*

Find the story in Daniel Chapter 6

Learn by heart: "*God loves you, so don't let anything worry you or frighten you.*" (Daniel 10:19)

Jonah and the big fish

Think carefully: *Have you ever been disobedient to God? The Bible teaches us to listen to what God asks us to do.*

Read: Jonah was a prophet. God asked him to go and warn the people of the city of Nineveh about their sinful lives. But Jonah did not want to do that. Instead of obeying God, he ran away and boarded a ship sailing to Tarshish.

God sent a wild storm to the sea so that the ship would sink. Jonah asked the sailors to throw him overboard because he knew that the storm was his fault. Jonah did not drown, because a big fish in the sea swallowed him. From inside the fish, Jonah prayed to God to save his life. God heard him and the fish spat Jonah out on dry land.

Jonah got such a fright that he immediately went to Nineveh to warn the people, as God had told him to do.

What God wants me to know:
It is not possible to run away from God. It is better to obey Him.

What I can say to God: *Lord, I am sorry that I sometimes do not want to do what You tell me to do. Please forgive me and help me to obey You. Amen.*

Find the story in Jonah Chapters 1 – 3

Learn by heart: *"I will do what I have promised."* (Jonah 2:9)

New Testament

The birth of Jesus

Think carefully: *What do you think about at Christmas time? Do you only think about the presents you are going to get, or are you happy that it is Jesus' birthday?*

Read: A young woman lived in Nazareth. Her name was Mary. One day, an angel told her that she would have a son. This son would be the Saviour that God had promised His people long ago.

When the baby was about to be born, Joseph and Mary were in Bethlehem. All the people had to go there to write their names in a book, because the king wanted to know how many people were in his land. Joseph and Mary could not find a place to sleep in Bethlehem. They eventually found a place in a stable.

In that stable Jesus, our Saviour, was born. Mary wrapped Him in cloths and placed Him in a manger.

What God wants me to know: *Jesus is God's precious gift to the world. We should be very happy about His birth so long ago.*

What I can say to God: *Lord Jesus, thank You that You were born in Bethlehem, so that I may become God's child. Thank You for Christmas, when we can celebrate Your birth. Amen.*

Find the story in Luke Chapter 2

Learn by heart: *"For God loved the world so much that he gave his only Son, so that everyone who believes in him may not die but have eternal life."* (John 3:16)

The shepherds receive the good news

Think carefully: *Do you like telling your parents and friends good news? Have you ever told anybody the good news about Jesus?*

Read: In the fields outside Bethlehem, shepherds were looking after their sheep. Suddenly a bright light shone over the fields and an angel said to the shepherds: "I bring you good news of great joy. Today in Bethlehem a Saviour has been born to you."

Suddenly a large group of angels appeared, praising God and saying: "Glory to God in the highest, and on earth peace to men on whom His favour rests."

When the angels left, the shepherds hurried to Bethlehem. They found the Child and His parents and knelt down to worship Him. They did not want to keep the news to themselves; they wanted to tell everyone that the Saviour was born.

What God wants me to know: *You must tell all your friends the good news about the birth of Jesus.*

What I can say to God: *Heavenly Father, thank You for sending Jesus to the world so that my sins may be forgiven. Help me to tell all my friends the good news. Amen.*

Find the story in Luke Chapter 2

Learn by heart: *"When the shepherds saw him, they told them what the angel had said about the child."* (Luke 2:17)

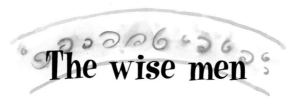

The wise men

Think carefully: *Do you think we can give Jesus presents? What would you like to give Him?*

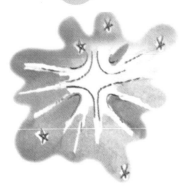

Read: Very far from Bethlehem there were wise men who noticed that there was a new, bright star in the sky. They knew that this meant that a great King had been born. The wise men packed gifts for the King and immediately got on their camels to go and look for Him.

In the little town of Bethlehem they saw the star above the stable where Joseph and Mary and the baby Jesus were. The wise men knelt before the new King and offered Him their gifts. They knew that He was the Saviour of the world and were very happy that they had found Him.

What God wants me to know: *The gift that God wants most of all is your heart.*

You can also give Jesus a present this Christmas that will make Him very happy. Give Him your heart.

What I can say to God: *Lord Jesus, I wish I could also give You presents like the wise men. I would like to give You my heart. Please forgive my sins so that I can be Your child. Amen.*

84

Find the story in Matthew Chapter 2

Learn by heart: *"They brought out their gifts of gold, frankincense, and myrrh, and presented them to him."* (Matthew 2:11)

The baptism of Jesus

 Think carefully: *Have you seen a baptism in your church?*

Read: John the Baptist lived in the desert and baptised people in the river Jordan. He told people that Jesus, the true Saviour, would soon appear.

One day Jesus went to the desert. When John saw Him, he knew immediately that Jesus was the Saviour. While John was baptising Jesus, the heavens opened and the Spirit of God came down like a dove and settled on Jesus.

God invites all people – men, women, boys, and girls – to trust Him to take care of them and to show them how to live. If we decide to trust Jesus and to obey Him, He promises to help us follow Him. One way He said we should let others know that we have decided to become a Christian is to be baptised. Have you decided to become a Christian? Have you been baptised?

What God wants me to know: *When you decide to become a Christian, you should follow Christ's example and be baptised. This lets everyone know about the decision you made.*

 What I can say to God: *Lord, thank you for giving me the choice to be Your child. Amen.*

 Find the story in Matthew Chapter 3

Learn by heart: *"Decide today whom you will serve."* (Joshua 24:15)

The story of a wedding

Think carefully: *What do you do when you have a problem? Do you ask Jesus to help you? Do you remember to thank Him?*

Read: Jesus and His mother went to a wedding banquet. In those days people celebrated a wedding for many days. After a while, all the wine was finished. Mary told Jesus: "Their wine is finished." Jesus asked: "Why do you tell Me?" But Mary knew that Jesus could help them. "Do whatever He tells you," Mary told the servants.

There were six stone jars at the wedding. "Fill the jars with water," Jesus told the servants. When they had done that, He said: "Now draw some out and take it to the master of the banquet." When the master of the banquet tasted the water that Jesus had changed into wine, he said: "The bridegroom has saved the good wine for last."

What God wants me to know: *Jesus can perform miracles. He can also help you when you have problems.*

What I can say to God: *Lord Jesus, thank You that You can do anything. I know You will also help me when I have problems. Amen.*

88

Find the story in John Chapter 2

Learn by heart: *"Our help comes from the Lord, who made heaven and earth."* (Psalm 124:8)

God takes care of the birds and the flowers

Think carefully: *Do you like picking flowers in the garden for your mother? Who do you think looks after the flowers and the birds and the animals?*

What God wants me to know: *You don't have to worry about anything. He will take care of you.*

Read: You must have heard that grownups have many things to worry about. Perhaps your mother has told you how expensive everything has become. These days it is very difficult to make ends meet.

If you belong to Jesus, you don't have to worry about what you are going to eat and drink, or where you are going to get clothes to wear. Jesus will take care of you, just as He takes care of the wild birds and animals and the flowers. All you have to do is to trust Him and to obey Him.

Jesus knows what you need. To Him, you are even more precious than the birds and flowers! He will look after you even better than He looks after them.

What I can say to God: *Heavenly Father, thank You for loving me and for giving me everything I need. Thank You that I don't need to worry and that I only have to trust You. Amen.*

Find the story in Matthew Chapter 6

Learn by heart: "*Your Father in heaven knows that you need all these things.*" (Matthew 6:32)

Jesus loves children

Think carefully: *Do you sometimes wish that you could see Jesus? That you could sit on His lap and feel His arms around you?*

Read: Jesus never got tired of talking to people who listened to Him. One day, some mothers brought their children to Jesus so that He could bless them. But Jesus' disciples scolded them and sent them away.

When Jesus saw this, He said: "Let the little children come to me, for the kingdom of God belongs to such as these." He put His arms around the children and blessed them. The grownups and disciples saw that Jesus loved children very much. They never kept children away from Him again.

Jesus still loves you as much as He loved those children in the story. Do you love Him too?

What God wants me to know: *Jesus loves children very much.*

What I can say to God: *Lord Jesus, I really wish I could see You and feel Your arms around me. Thank You for loving me so much. Amen.*

 Find the story in Mark Chapter 10

Learn by heart: *"Let the children come to Me, and do not stop them."*
(Mark 10:14)

The Lord's day

? **Think carefully:** *What do you do on Sundays? Do you enjoy going to church and Sunday school?*

Read: The Pharisees were people who obeyed the laws of God, but in their hearts they did not really love God. They had a great many rules and eventually these rules became more important to them than God Himself.

One Sunday, Jesus and His disciples were walking through the cornfields. They were hungry and began to pick some ears of corn to eat. The Pharisees made a big fuss about that. But Jesus told them that He was Lord over the Sabbath. Jesus also healed a man with a paralysed hand on a Sunday.

Sunday is not a day full of do's and don'ts. It is the day we must set aside for God, the day to busy ourselves with His work and the day to worship Him.

! **What God wants me to know:** *Sunday is God's special day during which we can spend time with Him.*

" **What I can say to God:** *Lord, thank You for Sundays. Thank You that I can go to church and Sunday school and talk about You with my friends. Amen.*

Find the story in Luke Chapter 6

Learn by heart: *"If you treat the Sabbath as sacred then you will find the joy that comes from serving me."* (Isaiah 58:13–14)

Bartimaeus can see again!

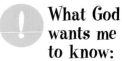

Think carefully: *Shut your eyes tightly. Now think of all the things you would not be able to see if you were blind.*

Read: Bartimaeus was a blind man. He believed that Jesus could heal him. One day, when he heard that Jesus was passing his way, he called out: "Jesus, have mercy on me!"

The people tried to silence him, but Bartimaeus ignored them. He called even more loudly: "Jesus, Son of David, help me!"

Jesus heard someone calling Him, and stopped immediately. "Bring the blind man here to Me," Jesus said. When Bartimaeus came to Jesus, He asked: "What do you want Me to do for you?" "Rabbi, I want to see," said Bartimaeus. Jesus answered: "Go. Your faith has healed you."

Then a miracle happened. For the first time in his life, Bartimaeus could see! He saw the people and the green grass and the blue sky. And he saw Jesus!

Jesus can still perform miracles if we have faith in Him.

What God wants me to know: *Jesus can do anything. He can make blind people see and sick people healthy.*

What I can say to God: *Lord Jesus, thank You that You can do anything. Thank You that You can make me better when I am ill. Amen.*

Find the story in Mark Chapter 10

Learn by heart: *"Everything is possible for God."* (Mark 10:27)

Jairus' little daughter

ISN IVISN

Think carefully: *Do you really believe that Jesus can make dead people live again? What happens to people who believe in God when they die?*

Read: Jairus was an official in the synagogue. His twelve-year-old daughter became very ill. Jairus went to look for Jesus and asked Him to heal his little daughter. Jesus went with Jairus to his home, but when they arrived there, the child had already died.

Jairus was very sad, but Jesus comforted him. "Do not be afraid, Jairus, just trust Me and I will help you," He said. Jesus sent all the people out of the house. Only the girl's parents and three of the disciples stayed behind. Then He took the little girl's hand and said: "Little girl, I say to you, get up." The little girl opened her eyes and sat up. Her parents were so happy.

Isn't Jesus wonderful?

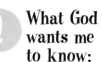

What God wants me to know:

If you believe in Jesus, you will rise from the dead one day and be with Him in heaven.

What I can say to God: *Lord Jesus, help me to believe that You can do anything, just as Jairus believed. I am grateful that I will be in heaven with You one day. Amen.*

Find the story in Mark Chapter 5 verses 21–42

Learn by heart: *"Whoever believes in me will live, even though he dies."*
(John 11:25)

Five loaves and two fish

Think carefully: *Would you be prepared to give Jesus everything you have so that He can use it?*

Read: One day, Jesus and His disciples rowed to a quiet place across the Sea of Galilee. They wanted to be alone, but thousands of people followed them. By evening, they were all tired and hungry, but there were no shops where they could buy food and the disciples did not have enough money to buy food for so many people.

One small boy brought Jesus five loaves of bread and two fish. Jesus took the food and, after He had prayed, He broke it into pieces. The disciples gave bread and fish to all the people. When they had all had enough to eat, there were still twelve baskets of bread and fish left!

You can also help Jesus if you share your things with other people like that little boy did.

What God wants me to know:

If you are prepared to give Jesus all the things you have, He can perform miracles with them.

What I can say to God: *Lord Jesus, help me to be willing to share what I have with other people. Thank You that You can perform miracles. Amen.*

Find the story in John Chapter 6

Learn by heart: *"I will show them my wonders."* (Micah 7:15 NIV)

Ten healed of leprosy

Think carefully: *Do you always remember to thank your mother when she does something for you? And do you thank God every day for the things He does for you and gives you?*

Read: Ten lepers lived outside Jerusalem. They were not allowed to come close to other people, because leprosy was most infectious. When Jesus walked past them, they called Him. "Jesus, please have pity on us," they asked Him.

Jesus felt sorry for them. "Go, show yourselves to the priests," He said. The ten immediately ran to the temple. As they ran, they saw that they were completely cured.

All the men were very happy to be cured, but only one man went back to thank Jesus. Jesus wondered where the other nine men were whom He had healed.

What God wants me to know:
You must always remember to thank God for everything He gives you and does for you.

What I can say to God: *Lord Jesus, I am very sorry that I sometimes forget to thank You for all the things You give to me. Help me always to be grateful. Amen.*

Find the story in Luke Chapter 17

Learn by heart: *"Be grateful for every year you live."* (Ecclesiastes 11:8)

The rich young man

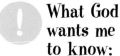

Think carefully: *What is the most important thing in your life? The one thing you would not exchange for anything?*

Read: One day there was a rich young man who came to listen to Jesus. "Good Teacher," he asked Jesus, "what must I do to inherit eternal life?"

"You know the commandments," Jesus told him. "These I have kept since I was a young boy," said the young man. Jesus looked at him and loved him. "Go, sell everything you have and give the money to the poor, then come, follow Me," Jesus said.

The young man went away sad, because he was not prepared to sell everything he owned. He was very rich and his money and possessions were more important to him than God was.

Jesus always wants to be the most important thing in His children's lives.

What God wants me to know: *If you want to follow Jesus, there must be nothing in your life that is more important to you than God.*

What I can say to God: *Lord Jesus, there are so many things that are important to me. But You are the most important of all. Thank You that I may love You. Amen.*

Find the story in Mark Chapter 10

Learn by heart: *"You, Lord, are all I have."* (Psalm 16:5)

Jesus teaches us to pray

 Think carefully: *Do you pray the same prayer day after day, or do you enjoy talking to Jesus? Do you know the Our Father prayer?*

Read: When Jesus was still on earth, He often went to a lonely place to pray. His disciples saw that He enjoyed talking to His Father, so they asked Him to teach them to pray.

Jesus taught them the Our Father prayer. With this prayer He wants to teach you how to talk to God. God is your Father who watches over you. He lives in heaven, but He is also here with you on earth. God cares for you and forgives your sins. He helps you to love other people. He is the great King to whom all power and glory belongs.

 What God wants me to know:
God is your Father who loves you–He wants you to talk to Him.

Wouldn't you like to learn the Our Father prayer by heart? You can read it in Matthew 6:9–13 in your Bible.

 What I can say to God: *Heavenly Father, thank You for letting me talk to You when I pray. Thank You for hearing and answering my prayers. Amen.*

106

Find the story in Luke Chapter 11

Learn by heart: *"If you ask me for anything in my name, I will do it."*
(John 14:14)

Ask, and you will receive

Think carefully: *Do you always receive everything you ask God for? Why doesn't He gives us everything that we ask for?*

Read: When you pray, you are talking to God. He is always there to listen to you. You can tell Him when you are happy or sad. You can thank Him for everything He gives you. You can praise and worship Him because He is wonderful. You can also ask Him for the things you really want.

But you have probably discovered that God does not give you everything you ask for, just as your mother doesn't give your baby brother the shiny breadknife when he cries for it. God knows when you ask for something that is not good for you, then He does not give it to you.

Next time you wonder why God did not give you what you asked for, remember that He always knows best. He only gives you what is good for you.

What God wants me to know: *God only gives you what is good for you, even if it is not exactly what you wanted.*

What I can say to God: *Heavenly Father, thank You that You know what I need. Please help me to ask You for things that are good for me. Amen.*

Find the story in Luke Chapter 11

Learn by heart: *"Ask, and you will receive."* (Matthew 7:7)

Give everything to Jesus

Think carefully: *Do you think £5 is too much money to put in the collection plate at church? Is £5 too much to pay for a movie?*

Read: One day, when Jesus was in the temple, He saw the rich people putting lots of money in the money box. He also saw a poor widow put two small coins in the box.

Jesus said to His disciples: "I tell you that this poor widow has put in more than all the others. All these people gave their gifts out of what they had to spare; but she, poor as she is, gave all she had to live on."

You can also give some of your money for God's work. It is strange that some people are quite happy to spend money on things like the movies or eating out, but when they have to give money for God's work, they only put small change in the collection plate.

What God wants me to know:

God is pleased when we give away our money for Him. It shows Him that we love Him.

What I can say to God: *Lord, I am sorry that I also put only my small change in the collection plate. Help me to be willing to give myself and my money for Your work. Amen.*

Find the story in Luke Chapter 21

Learn by heart: *"God loves the one who gives gladly."*
(2 Corinthians 9:7)

Do as Jesus does

Think carefully: *What kind of work does your school caretaker do? Would you be prepared to do everything he or she does?*

Read: Just before Jesus' death, He celebrated the Last Supper with His disciples. When everyone was seated around the table, Jesus stood up, took a bowl of water, and began to wash His disciples' feet. Jesus was their Lord and Master, but He was willing to do the work of a slave because He loved them.

Jesus wants us to follow His example. "Now that you know these things, you will be blessed if you do them," He said to His disciples.

Are you prepared to serve and help others as Jesus did? Then you can start right now. Today!

What God wants me to know: *You must be willing to serve and help other people.*

What I can say to God: *Lord, sometimes I am very lazy when I have to help others. Make me willing and ready to follow Your example. Amen.*

Find the story in John Chapter 13

Learn by heart: *"If one of you wants to be great, he must be the servant of the rest."* (Mark 10:43)

Forgive one another

 Think carefully: *What do you do when a friend makes you very angry and later asks for your forgiveness?*

Read: One day there was a man who owed the king millions of pounds. He would never be able to pay it back. The king wanted to have him thrown into prison, but then felt sorry for him and wrote off all his debts.

But do you know what that man did? One of his friends owed him a few thousand pounds. He grabbed the man and said: "Pay the money you owe me immediately!" The man begged for some time, but he wouldn't listen and had him thrown in prison. When the king heard this, he was so angry that he punished the man until he paid off all his debts.

God is always prepared to forgive you your debts, but He expects you to forgive other people when they hurt you.

What God wants me to know: *God forgives you your sins, but He also wants you to forgive other people who make you angry.*

 What I can say to God: *Heavenly Father, thank You that You are always prepared to forgive me my sins. Help me to forgive the people who make me angry. Amen.*

 Find the story in Matthew Chapter 18

Learn by heart: *"If you forgive others the wrongs they have done to you, your Father in heaven will also forgive you."* (Matthew 6:14)

Jesus sends the Holy Spirit

Think carefully: *Would you be able to explain to one of your friends who the Holy Spirit is? Or are you a little confused?*

Read: The disciples were very sad when Jesus told them that He was returning to His Father in heaven. "Do not be worried and upset because I am leaving you," Jesus told them. "I will send Someone in My place. His name is the Holy Spirit. He will stay with you forever and He will teach you about Me. He will comfort you when you are sad. He will help you to tell others about Me."

The Holy Spirit is God. He lives in every child of God, and in you. He tells you if you do things that are wrong and He teaches you to pray. He teaches you to understand the Bible. He is the One who helps you know in your heart that you are God's child.

Has this helped you to understand who the Holy Spirit is?

What God wants me to know: *The Holy Spirit lives in you. You are God's temple!*

What I can say to God: *Holy Spirit, thank You that You live in me. Thank You for telling me when I am wrong, for teaching me to pray, and for helping me to understand that I am God's child. Amen.*

Find the story in John Chapters 14 – 16

Learn by heart: *"Surely you know that you are God's temple and that God's Spirit lives in you!"* (1 Corinthians 3:16)

117

The Holy Spirit teaches you to pray

Think carefully: *Perhaps there are times when you don't really know what to say when you pray. What can you do when this happens?*

Read: It is not always easy to pray. Some nights you may be too sleepy to pray. You almost fall asleep while you are praying. Or you may be in such a hurry to get to school that you don't have enough time to talk to God. Or you just recite exactly the same prayer every day: "God bless Mum and Dad and Grandma and Grandad..."

When this happens to you, ask the Holy Spirit to help you. He helps us to pray when we don't know what to say to God. Romans 8:26 tells us that He prays without words.

Next time you find it hard to pray, ask the Holy Spirit to help you. He will help you each time you ask Him.

What God wants me to know: *The Holy Spirit teaches you how to pray.*

What I can say to God: *Holy Spirit, thank You that You want to teach me to pray. Please give me the right words when I want to talk to God. Amen.*

Find the story in Romans Chapter 8 verses 26–28

Learn by heart: *"The Spirit himself pleads with God for us.*
(Romans 8:26)

119

You must be a witness

Think carefully: *Do you find it difficult to talk to your friends about Jesus? Do you like praying aloud at a family meal, or are you too shy?*

Read: Paul's life task was to tell people who had not heard of Jesus about Him. He was one of the greatest witnesses ever. Today there are still witnesses, called missionaries, who work in other countries and tell the people there about Jesus. But it is not necessary to go to a faraway country to be a witness. You can do it right here where you live, by talking to friends and other people about Jesus.

Jesus wants every one of His children to be a witness for Him. "You are to tell others what you have seen of Me today and what I will show you in the future," He said to Paul (Acts 26:16). Paul listened to Jesus and spent the rest of his life telling people who did not know God the good news about Him. Do you do this too?

What God wants me to know: *Every one of God's children must be a witness for Him.*

What I can say to God: *Lord Jesus, sometimes I am too shy to talk about You to my friends. Please help me to be Your witness. Amen.*

Find the story in Acts Chapter 26

Learn by heart: *"But when the Holy Spirit comes upon you, you will be filled with power, and you will be witnesses for me."* (Acts 1:8)

121

Peter is sorry

Think carefully: *Have you ever done something about which you were very sorry? What made you feel better?*

Read: Peter loved Jesus, but he was also very scared. When the Roman soldiers took Jesus away, Peter swore three times that he did not know Jesus. After the third time, a cock crowed.

Suddenly, Peter remembered that Jesus had told him he would betray Him three times before the cock crowed. Peter was terribly sad and sorry. He went outside and sobbed.

Because Jesus knew that Peter was sorry that he had betrayed Him, He forgave Peter.

If you do something you are very sorry about, Jesus will forgive you, too, when you ask Him.

What God wants me to know: *If you are sorry that you have sinned, God will always forgive you.*

What I can say to God: *Lord Jesus, I am sorry I often do the wrong thing. Thank You that You always forgive me. Amen.*

Find the story in John Chapters 18, 21

Learn by heart: "*You are a God who forgives.*" (Nehemiah 9:17)

When we take communion

Think carefully: *Have you ever watched the grownups taking communion in church? Do you know what the bread and wine mean?*

Read: Jesus and His disciples went to Jerusalem to celebrate the Passover. While they were eating the Passover meal, Jesus took some of the bread and gave each disciple a piece. "When you eat this bread," He said, "remember that I died so that your sins can be forgiven."

Then He took the cup of wine and offered it to each of them. "This wine is like My blood," Jesus said. He meant that His blood would flow on the cross so that our sins may be forgiven.

When we take communion and eat the bread, we think of Jesus' body that was broken on the cross. When we drink the wine we think of how Jesus' blood flowed when He died on the cross for us.

What God wants me to know:

You must remember Jesus' body and blood when you take communion— until He comes again.

What I can say to God: *Lord Jesus, thank You for being prepared to die on the cross so that my sins may be forgiven. Thank You for helping me to understand what communion means. Amen.*

Find the story in Mark Chapter 14

Learn by heart: *"Every time you eat this bread and drink from this cup you proclaim the Lord's death."* (1 Corinthians 11:26)

Jesus is crucified

 Think carefully: *Have you ever been punished for something you didn't do? Would you like it if you were punished for something your brother or sister did?*

Read: God loves us very much, but He hates sin and He always punishes sin with death. We are all sinners and therefore deserve to die. There is not one person on earth who is without sin.

You and I are also sinners and deserve God's punishment. But because God loves us so much, He sent His Son Jesus to die on the cross for us. By doing that, Jesus paid the price of all our sins for us. Jesus saved us by giving up His life for us. He was punished for the wrong we do.

Because Jesus paid the price of our sins on the cross, God forgives us for our sins, and we can be God's children.

What God wants me to know: *Jesus paid the price of your sin when He died on the cross.*

What I can say to God: *Lord Jesus, how can I thank You for being prepared to die for me? Help me to live for You from now on. Amen.*

 Find the story in Luke Chapter 23

Learn by heart: *"We are healed by the punishment he suffered."*
(Isaiah 53:5)

127

Jesus rose from the dead

Think carefully: *Has someone died whom you loved very much? How did you feel?*

Read: After Jesus had been crucified, His friends took His body from the cross and placed it in a new tomb in a garden near Gethsemane. They rolled a large stone in front of the opening of the tomb.

The next day, when Mary Magdalene arrived at the tomb, she saw that the stone had been rolled away and that the tomb was empty. Mary was very sad. She stood at the tomb and cried. Suddenly she heard a voice asking: "Why are you crying?"

Thinking it was the gardener, she said: "Sir, if you have carried Him away, tell me where you have put Him." Then she saw that the man she was talking to was Jesus Himself! Mary was very happy. She immediately went and told everybody the good news that Jesus had risen from the dead.

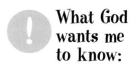

What God wants me to know: *Jesus rose from the dead. He lives!*

What I can say to God: *Lord Jesus, thank You that You rose from the dead and that You will live forever. Thank You that I can be in heaven with You one day. Amen.*

Find the story in John Chapter 20

Learn by heart: *"He is not here; he has been raised."* (Luke 24:6)

Jesus will come again

Think carefully: *Have you ever wondered what will happen when Jesus comes again? Are you ready to follow Him?*

Read: After Jesus had promised His disciples for the last time that He would send them the Holy Spirit, a cloud came and took Him away before their eyes. While the disciples were staring into the sky as He was leaving them, two men dressed in white suddenly stood beside them.

"This Jesus, who was taken from you into heaven, will come back in the same way that you saw Him go to heaven," the men told the disciples.

If you belong to Jesus, it is good to know that He will return one day. When He comes, He will take all His children here on earth so that they will live with Him in heaven forever. Make sure that you will be ready to go with Him.

What God wants me to know: *Jesus will come to take you to live with Him in heaven forever.*

What I can say to God: *Lord Jesus, thank You for the promise that You will return to earth. Help me to live in such a way that I will be ready when You come. Amen.*

Find the story in Acts Chapter 1

Learn by heart: *"Jesus will come back in the same way that you saw him go to heaven."* (Acts 1:11)

Pray with others

Think carefully: *Do you and your friends enjoy praying together? Why or why not?*

Read: After Jesus had gone to heaven, His disciples stayed behind in Jerusalem. They all prayed together, as Jesus had asked them to do. On the day of Pentecost they heard a sound like a strong wind. Something like tongues of fire came to rest on them. They were all filled with the Holy Spirit and began to speak in other languages.

Peter spoke to the crowd, asking them to repent and to be baptised. On that day about 3,000 people gave their hearts to the Lord! This was the result of the disciples' prayers. When people pray together, God hears their prayers.

What God wants me to know:
Jesus wants His children to pray together. He has promised that He will listen to them.

What I can say to God: *Lord Jesus, I am sorry that I am sometimes too shy to pray with my friends. Help me not to be shy. Amen.*

Find the story in Acts Chapters 1 - 2

Learn by heart: "*For where two or three come together in my name, I am there with them.*" (Matthew 18:20)

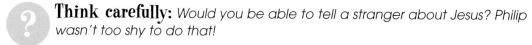

Philip and the Ethiopian

? Think carefully: *Would you be able to tell a stranger about Jesus? Philip wasn't too shy to do that!*

Read: One day, an important Ethiopian was on his way from Jerusalem to Gaza. He was reading from the book of Isaiah the prophet, but he could not understand what he was reading.

Then God sent Philip to the man. When he saw that the strange man was reading the book of Isaiah, Philip asked him: "Do you understand what you are reading?"

! What God wants me to know: *God loves everybody, even those who do not know Him yet.*

The Ethiopian invited Philip to climb up and sit in the chariot with him and to explain the Scripture to him. Philip told him all about Jesus. When they drove past some water, the Ethiopian asked Philip to baptise him. He believed in Jesus, so Philip baptised him. This made the Ethiopian very happy.

" What I can say to God: *Lord, make me willing to tell strangers about You. Thank You that I can understand the Bible. Amen.*

134

Find the story in Acts Chapter 8

Learn by heart: *"Whoever calls out to the Lord for help will be saved."*
(Acts 2:21)

The Lord gives us what we ask for

Think carefully: *Have you ever asked God for something you wanted very badly? What did you do when He gave it to you?*

Read: King Herod had Peter thrown into prison. The whole church prayed to have him released from prison.

While Peter was in prison, God sent an angel to him. The angel led Peter out of the prison. Peter immediately went to the house of Mary, the mother of John. There he found people still praying for him.

When the servant girl opened the door, she thought Peter was a ghost! The people did not want to believe her when she told them that Peter was standing at the door. Isn't it strange that we sometimes ask God for something and then can't believe that He has answered our prayers?

What God wants me to know: *When people pray according to God's will, He always answers their prayers.*

What I can say to God: *Lord, I'm sorry that I sometimes pray for something but don't really believe that You will give it to me. Please make my faith stronger. Amen.*

Find the story in Acts Chapter 12 verses 1–19

Learn by heart: *"Be persistent in prayer."* (Colossians 4:2)

Paul and Barnabas

? **Think carefully:** *Have you ever been made team captain? How do you feel when someone chooses you to do something special?*

Read: In the city of Antioch many people believed in Jesus. The Holy Spirit told them to choose Paul and Barnabas to work for Him. Paul and Barnabas were very willing to do that. First of all they went to the island of Cyprus to tell the people there about Jesus.

For twenty years Paul travelled through the world and told people everywhere the good news about Jesus. He preached in churches and palaces, in houses and in prisons. He spoke to ordinary people and soldiers, and to kings and prisoners. He never forgot that God had chosen him to spread the good news. God still wants all His children to be His witnesses.

Would you be willing, like Paul, to tell other people about Jesus?

! **What God wants me to know:** *God has chosen you to be His witness.*

" **What I can say to God:** *Heavenly Father, thank You for choosing me to be Your child and witness. Please help me to do what You ask. Amen.*

Find the story in Acts Chapter 13

Learn by heart: *"I chose you and appointed you to go."*
(John 15:16)

139

Are you afraid?

Think carefully: *Is there something you are really afraid of? What do you do when you are scared?*

Read: Timothy was a young boy who knew Jesus. His mother and grandmother had told him about Jesus from a young age. Paul loved Timothy very much. He asked Timothy to help him with his missionary work. At first Timothy was very scared, but Paul encouraged him. "God did not give us a spirit that makes us afraid, but a spirit of power and love and self-control," Paul told him.

God wants His children to be brave. When Timothy asked God to help him, he was no longer afraid. He travelled with Paul and told people about Jesus.

When you are afraid, you can tell Jesus all about your fears and ask Him to take away your fears. He will make you just as brave as Timothy.

What God wants me to know: *God is always with you when you are afraid.*

What I can say to God: *Lord, I am grateful that You will always be with me. Thank You that You will help me to be brave. Amen.*

 Find the story in 2 Timothy Chapter 1

Learn by heart: "*Do not be afraid—I am with you!*" (Isaiah 43:5)

Published in the UK in 2002 by Candle Books
(a publishing imprint of Lion Hudson plc)
Reprinted 2002, 2004
Distributed by Marston Book Services Ltd, PO Box 269, Abingdon, Oxon OX14 4YN

ISBN 1 85985 422 2

Primary source of Scripture quotations from the Good News Bible, with permissions. Quotations
marked NIV are taken from New International Version © 1973, 1978, 1984 by International Bible
Society. Used by permission.

Worldwide co-edition organised and produced by Lion Hudson plc
Mayfield House, 256 Banbury Road, Oxford OX2 7DH
Tel: +44 (0) 1865 302750 Fax: +44 (0) 1865 302757
Email: coed@lionhudson.com www.lionhudson.com

Printed in Singapore